# WINSLOW HOMER'S

# AMERICA

# WINSLOW HOMER'S

Lloyd Goodrich

# AMERICA

Tudor Publishing Co.     New York

# Foreword

WINSLOW HOMER WAS NOT ONLY one of the foremost American painters of his time, but also one of our leading illustrators. Since the beginning of my research and writing on his life and art, over thirty years ago, I have planned some day to do a book on his illustrations. I wish to express my gratitude to Shorewood Publishers for the opportunity to present in this volume the best graphic creations of this major artist.

This book is based on a study of Homer's works in all mediums—oils, watercolors, drawings, prints, and illustrations—which I have carried on in preparation for a complete catalogue raisonné of his lifework. This study has involved extensive examination of the illustrated periodicals and books of Homer's time. Pioneer research in this field was embodied in Allen Evarts Foster's two checklists of Homer's illustrations in periodicals (*Bulletin of the New York Public Library*, October, 1936, and July, 1940). Several additions to Mr. Foster's lists have been made possible by further search of periodicals, by fuller biographical information, and by comparison with works by Homer in other mediums, which establish his authorship of certain unsigned illustrations.

The works selected for reproduction in the present book represent about one third of Homer's published illustrations. They have been chosen both for their value as works of art and for their interest as pictorial records of American life. A complete list of Homer's illustrations in periodicals and books, and of his lithographs and etchings, will be included in my catalogue raisonné.

For constant assistance in this as in all matters connected with Winslow Homer, I want to record my indebtedness to my wife and fellow researcher, Edith Havens Goodrich.

# Contents

# The Young Illustrator

WINSLOW HOMER WAS ONE OF THE MOST VITAL American artists of the nineteenth century, and a pioneer in the realistic picturing of the American scene. He saw aspects of contemporary life in the United States that no previous artist had seen, and he depicted them with perennial freshness and vigor. Throughout his long, active career he covered a wide range of subjects and passed through many successive stages in his growth as an artist. While he is most famous for his great oil paintings and watercolors of the sea and the wilderness, he also created in his earlier work a unique pictorial record of American life in the 1860's and 1870's. An important part of this record is his work as an illustrator, which forms one of the liveliest chapters in American art.

Homer began his career as a graphic artist; it was not until his late twenties that he started to be a painter. His early experience as an illustrator played an essential part in his development by training his eye and hand to observe things and to record them swiftly and surely. The basis of all his work, from his first drawings to his last paintings, was draftsmanship.

Homer was a New Englander by birth and long ancestry, descended from Captain John Homer, shipmaster, who had settled in Boston in the seventeenth century. It was in Boston that Winslow Homer was born, in 1836. Growing up in nearby Cambridge, which was still no more than a big village, he had an active outdoor boyhood that left him with a lifelong love of the country. As a youth he was independent and strong willed, little given to talk, and he had a dry Yankee sense of humor.

As an artist he was almost entirely self-taught. Instead of going to an art school he was apprenticed at nineteen to a Boston lithographer, John H. Bufford. In Bufford's shop he drew illustrated covers for sheet music, portraits of leading citizens (from photographs), and other banalities. He hated the drudgery of his job. He had already decided to be a painter some day, and in the meantime to make his living as an illustrator. When his apprenticeship was over, on his twenty-first birthday, he left Bufford's and launched himself on the career of a free-lance illustrator.

At this time the leading illustrated weekly magazine in Boston was *Ballou's Pictorial Drawing-Room Companion,* with a circulation—large for the time—of over a hundred thousand. A contemporary writer described the *Pictorial* and other Ballou publications as "beautiful specimens of art and pleasing and pure caskets of literature." "Mr. Ballou," he added, "never admits an indelicate allusion, an innuendo of doubtful tendency, or aught else that can corrupt, to find its way into the columns of his paper. . . . These publications may be placed in the hands of the wife, the daughter, the son, or any within the sacred circle of home, in perfect confidence that their effect will only prove salutary. Of how few publications can we thus speak." And indeed, compared to such rowdy New York magazines as *Frank Leslie's Illustrated Newspaper* or the *New-York Illustrated News, Ballou's Pictorial* was singularly pure. Instructive articles on foreign lands, biographies of irreproachable public figures, and fiction of unquestionable propriety were to be found in it, but the controversial field of politics was shunned, crime news was taboo, and there was absolutely no humor aside from a weekly column of immaculate puns.

Today most magazine illustrations are made from photographs, but in the 1850's, 1860's, and 1870's almost all illustrations were produced by artists. The process of reproduction itself was also entirely by hand. Today the artist's work is translated by photomechanical methods into the minute dots or lines of the printing plate, but in Homer's time the usual method was wood-engraving. A wooden block—boxwood, because of its extremely fine grain—was polished and then coated with white, making a smooth surface almost like paper. On this the artist drew his picture, in reverse (that is, right was left). The block was then turned over to an engraver who cut away the bare white surface, leaving the artist's drawn lines in relief. When inked and printed, the block gave a reproduction of the original drawing, translated into the black lines of the wood-block. The drawing itself, of course, had been destroyed piecemeal in the process of engraving. The functions of artist and engraver were entirely separate. As far as we know, Homer never engraved a block himself.

Judging by the style of his illustrations, and by the existing preliminary sketches that he did for them, Homer probably drew on the block in pencil and ink wash, producing a drawing that was practically a black-and-white watercolor. Many magazine illustrators, especially reportorial artists, often sent in sketches on paper, to be redrawn by staff artists. Homer seldom did this; the pronounced difference between his usual illustrations and the few redrawn by others is evidence that he almost always drew directly on the block.

Homer's first contribution to *Ballou's* was a portrait, published June 6, 1857, drawn from either a photograph or a sketch by another artist; thereafter a good half of his production for the magazine was hackwork of this kind. But at the same time he was doing more original illustrations. The week following his debut, there appeared a lively street scene near Ballou's office, "drawn expressly for us by Mr. Winslow Homer, a promising young artist of this city." This was the first of a series of Boston scenes representing the picturesque aspects of everyday city life as no previous illustrator had done, and introducing a new note of realism and humor into the stodgy pages of *Ballou's*. The scenes were easily recognizable to Bostonians, and the young artist carefully lettered all the familiar shop signs.

In the meantime a new illustrated magazine had been started in New York—*Harper's Weekly*. Backed by the great house of Harper, numbering among its authors Dickens, Wilkie Collins, Charles Reade, and Bulwer-Lytton, attracting the best illustrators, and opening its columns to humorous drawings and political cartoons, it soon became the leading publication of its kind in the country, the one indispensable magazine for the library table of every well-regulated American home. A few months after its founding, Homer submitted some drawings of life at Harvard, including what was described as a "foot-ball" match—in which several players were wearing top hats. The illustrations were accepted and published in August, 1857, and thereafter *Harper's* took almost everything he submitted, usually giving him full pages, sometimes double pages, and often the cover page. *Ballou's*, while always referring to "our artist" in the most flattering terms, only once allowed him more than a half page, so that while continuing to draw for them he was soon sending more and better work to *Harper's*.

The early pictures for both magazines were Boston scenes—the fashionable world promenading on Washington Street, or women and children on the Common. In all of them the accent was on elegance. The women were pretty and stylish in their crinolines, the strutting males imposing in top hats and curling side-whiskers. Occasionally there might be a glimpse of the seamier side of city life, but the usual emphasis was on its pleasant aspects.

The country around Boston furnished other subjects—riding, picnicking, and bathing in summer, in winter skating and sleighing. Again the elegant note was stressed. The inevitable top hat accompanied the young men on picnics, and the young ladies remained fashionable even when fleeing from snakes. The beau at the seashore, scaring the girls with a lobster, did not abandon his cane. The artist exploited to the full the decorative possibilities of hoopskirts blown by the breeze or agitated by some small accident, and there was always a discreetly revealed ankle. At least one handsome couple was usually shown tête-à-tête. But the prevailing tone was less of sentiment than of innocent gaiety, with crowds of children giving the outings a family air.

Soon Homer branched out into homelier scenes of New England farm life—harvesttime, Thanksgiving and Christmas celebrations, rustic dances, family gatherings with cider-drinking before huge open fires. In a cornhusking festival a lucky swain uncovers a red ear and claims his prize of a kiss; in an apple bee a girl throws a paring over her shoulder to see if it will form her lover's initial. Such pictures captured the flavor of American country life as few illustrators had done.

He began to travel outside of Boston for subjects: to Newport to draw the bathing, to West Point for a cadet "hop." For *Ballou's* he made a trip to Cape Cod to cover a religious camp meeting; one picture shows himself standing—short, slender, dapper—outside a tent, coolly sketching the weeping, ranting sinners within.

American illustration of the time was still strongly influenced by English publications. *Punch* and the *London Illustrated News* served as models for our magazines. In the absence of international copyright, even *Harper's Weekly* had no compunction about pirating their pictures, simply re-engraving them, so that Leech, Keene, Du Maurier, and Tenniel were as familiar here as our own Darley. Because he had been brought up in this generic Anglo-American style, Homer's first illustrations were little different from any other artist's, and without his signature they would be hard to pick out. But soon he began to develop a style at once more personal and more native, and his drawings stood out from the others. Their observation was fresher, their draftsmanship abler. The line was bold and incisive, its vitality surviving even the deadening process of engraving. There was always a sense of movement, and an energy that made other illustrators seem tame. Strong contrasts of black and white made his illustrations livelier than the dreary grayness of most wood-engravings.

In the fall of 1859, halfway through his twenty-fourth year, he left Boston to seek his fortune in New York, now the art and publishing center of the country. Because of the competition of *Harper's* and other New York rivals, *Ballou's* was about to give up illustrations, leaving Boston without an illustrated paper. "We recall with satisfaction," wrote Mr. Ballou in his valedictory, "the fact that we have never printed a vulgarism, or outraged sensibility by introducing low caricatures, or an indelicate allusion."

In leaving Boston, Homer did not break his ties with his birthplace; he visited it frequently and for years spent part of each summer with his parents, now settled in Belmont outside the city. New England, the land of his childhood, was the land to which he most loved to return, and in later life he was to return to it for good.

The Harpers made him a generous offer to enter their employ as a staff artist. "I declined it," Homer later told an interviewer, "because I had had a taste of freedom. The slavery at Bufford's was too fresh in my recollection to let me care to bind myself again. From the time that I took my nose off that lithographic stone, I have had no master; and never shall have any." *13*

But he continued to work for the magazine as a free lance. The double-page Christmas drawing for 1859 was his, and in it for the first time we recognize New York scenes—the fashionable residents of the fine brownstone mansions of lower Fifth Avenue contrasted with the Irish squatters and goats of Fifty-ninth Street. Other pictures of the city in winter followed, notably the delightful "Skating on the Ladies' Skating-pond in the Central Park, New York." The text explained that the lakes were divided into the Ladies' Pond and the Gentlemen's Pond; in the former "no gentlemen are allowed to skate unless they are accompanied by ladies." Looking at this swirl of fashion we marvel at the fortitude of our ancestors, who added to the natural difficulty of skating that of doing it in hoopskirts, and with top hats and canes. He also began to copy portraits from photographs for *Harper's,* as he had done for *Ballou's,* signing them simply "H," evidently not being proud of them.

As time passed he got to know other artists. After two years of living in boardinghouses, he moved to the New York University Building on Washington Square, where several of them lived. His brother Charles later described a night scene in his studio: a dozen artists and friends are in the room; Homer, busy on a drawing for *Harper's* that had to be done by midnight, sitting on the model stand and working away in the midst of a hubbub of talk and storytelling, shouts, "Here, one of you chaps, fill my pipe for me! I'm too busy to stop."

# The Young Illustrator

THE FOUNTAIN ON BOSTON COMMON    *Ballou's Pictorial Drawing-Room Companion*    August 15, 1857

COASTING OUT OF DOORS
*Ballou's Pictorial Drawing-Room Companion*
November 28, 1857

18

FAMILY PARTY PLAYING AT FOX AND GEESE
*Ballou's Pictorial Drawing-Room Companion*
November 28, 1857

BLINDMAN'S BUFF
*Ballou's Pictorial Drawing-Room Companion*
November 28, 1857

HUSKING PARTY FINDING THE RED EARS
*Ballou's Pictorial Drawing-Room Companion*
November 28, 1857

THE MATCH BETWEEN SOPHS AND FRESHMEN—THE OPENING  *Harper's Weekly*  August 1, 1857

21

THE BOSTON COMMON     *Harper's Weekly*     May 22, 1858

CLASS DAY, AT HARVARD UNIVERSITY, CAMBRIDGE, MASS.    *Ballou's Pictorial Drawing-Room Companion*    July 3, 1858

23

LANDING AT THE CAPE
*Ballou's Pictorial Drawing-Room Companion*
August 21, 1858

24

COOKING
*Ballou's Pictorial Drawing-Room Companion*
August 21, 1858

MORNING ABLUTIONS
*Ballou's Pictorial Drawing-Room Companion*
August 21, 1858

THE TENT
*Ballou's Pictorial Drawing-Room Companion*
August 21, 1858

25

PICNICKING IN THE WOODS     *Harper's Weekly*     September 4, 1858

THE BATHE AT NEWPORT    *Harper's Weekly*    September 4, 1858

CHRISTMAS—GATHERING EVERGREENS    *Harper's Weekly*    December 25, 1858

SKATING ON JAMAICA POND, NEAR BOSTON
*Ballou's Pictorial Drawing-Room Companion*
January 29, 1859

30

EVENING SCENE AT THE SKATING PARK, BOSTON
*Ballou's Pictorial Drawing-Room Companion*
March 12, 1859

SKATING ON THE LADIES' SKATING-POND IN THE CENTRAL PARK, NEW YORK    *Harper's Weekly*    **January 28, 1860**

31

32

BOSTON STREET CHARACTERS
*Ballou's Pictorial Drawing-Room Companion*
July 9, 1859

CAMBRIDGE CATTLE MARKET
*Ballou's Pictorial Drawing-Room Companion*
July 2, 1859

FOURTH OF JULY SCENE, ON BOSTON COMMON
*Ballou's Pictorial Drawing-Room Companion*
July 9, 1859

33

34

AUGUST IN THE COUNTRY—THE SEA-SHORE   *Harper's Weekly*   August 27, 1859

35

A CADET HOP AT WEST POINT    *Harper's Weekly*    September 3, 1859

36

MAY-DAY IN THE COUNTRY    *Harper's Weekly*    April 30, 1859

THE SLEIGHING SEASON—THE UPSET     *Harper's Weekly*     January 14, 1860

A Snow Slide in the City    *Harper's Weekly*    January 14, 1860

A Merry Christmas and Happy New Year     *Harper's Weekly*     December 24, 1859

41

THE DRIVE IN THE CENTRAL PARK, NEW YORK, SEPTEMBER, 1860    *Harper's Weekly*    September 15, 1860

POLICEMAN. "Lost anything, Sir?"
EXASPERATED OLD PARTY. "Don't you see that I've lost my hat?"
POLICEMAN. "Describe it."

SCENE IN UNION SQUARE, NEW YORK, ON A MARCH DAY     *Harper's Weekly*     April 7, 1860

# The Civil War

HOMER'S EARLY ILLUSTRATIONS had nothing to do with public affairs. But this was to change with the momentous events of 1861. When Lincoln passed through New York on his way to be inaugurated, Homer drew him addressing the people from the balcony of the Astor House. Commissioned by *Harper's* to cover the inauguration, he went to Washington and did a two-page drawing of the new president making his inaugural speech before the huge crowd in front of the Capitol.

When the war broke out there was a great demand for news pictures. *Harper's* sent out several special artists, one to cover each army. These men lived soldiers' lives, constantly with the troops, following every battle, and sending back drawings to the magazine each week, often with written accounts. As *Harper's* said at the end of the war: "They have shared the soldier's fare; they have ridden and waded, and climbed and floundered. . . . The pictorial history of the war which they have written with their pencils in the field, upon their knees, upon a knapsack, upon a bulwark, upon a drum-head, upon a block, upon a canteen, upon a wet deck, in the gray dawn, in the dusk twilight, with freezing or fevered fingers . . . —this is a history quivering with life, faithful, terrible, romantic."

Homer was a war artist of this kind only for brief periods. He made several trips to the front and saw some fighting, but he was not stationed permanently with the armies. Most of his war drawings, based on what he had seen with the troops, were done back in New York, and were of general phases of army life rather than specific events. This was due not to any lack of talent for reportorial drawing, but doubtless to his independence, his aversion to being tied down to a steady job, and his ambition to be something more than an illustrator.

The first six months of the war he seems to have spent in New York, and in the summer, as usual, at his parents' home in Belmont. While the regular military artists were wading through Virginia mud, he was drawing his pretty Belmont cousins and their friends sewing havelocks for the soldiers. What was probably his first visit to the front was made in October, 1861, as a special artist for *Harper's*, detailed to the Army of the Potomac. At this time all was very quiet along the Potomac. Since its humiliating defeat at Bull Run a few months earlier, the army had remained in camp outside Washington, undergoing a rigorous reorganization under General McClellan. Homer could have seen no fighting on this visit, which lasted no more than a few weeks, but he made enough sketches to do several illustrations after his return to New York.

His war illustrations, at this time and later, seldom pictured actual fighting. They were mostly of the everyday life in camp that made up nine-tenths of a soldier's existence, with its rough humor and simple pastimes—soldiers gathered around a bivouac fire at night, watching a Negro dance while another plays a banjo, the dramatic lights and shadows contrasting with the remote glow of the moon; the interior of a hut lit by a roaring fire, men sleeping on the floor, a few restless souls playing cards and quarrelling; soldiers on payday descending on a sutler's tent and gorging themselves on pie, salt herring, and cider, or at Christmas opening boxes from loving families, falling on the food and socks, tossing the tracts aside. Here were authentic types of a democratic army—gaunt Yankees looking like Uncle Sam, bulldog Irishmen from New York, swaggering Zouaves in exotic uniforms, with curling moustaches and imperials—hard specimens all, drawn with humor and keen characterization, and contrasting with the waxwork heroes pictured by other illustrators. Drinking, fighting, gambling and crude horseplay were not soft-pedalled, but on the whole the picture Homer drew of military life was jovial rather than sardonic. No other illustrator left so authentic a record of how the Civil War soldier really looked and acted. The nearest equivalent in our literature was not to appear for thirty years: Stephen Crane's *Red Badge of Courage*.

In the same vein, but with broader emphasis on the humorous side of army life, was a series of six lithographs, *Campaign Sketches,* published by the Boston lithographer Louis Prang in 1863. Drawn directly on the stone by Homer, they have the graphic freshness and richness that were often lost in the wood-engraving process. Next year came a sequel, *Life in Camp,* twenty-four small lithographed postcards more obviously comic and cruder in style. "Our Special" is a burlesque self-portrait, and in "Good Bye" Homer cast himself as the departing soldier.

Occasionally he did large designs of a more general inspirational character, such as "Songs of the War" and "News from the War"—many scenes tied together by appropriate decorative motifs. Intended to appeal to patriotism, these were essentially cartoons. As such they were not entirely successful, for Homer was too objective and dryly humorous to make a good propagandist. It remained for Thomas Nast to do the same thing for *Harper's* much more effectively, and to earn Lincoln's comment, "Nast has been our best recruiting sergeant."

In the spring of 1862 Homer made another trip to the front and this time saw more action. The long-awaited offensive against Richmond was about to be launched. McClellan's Army of the Potomac, the most formidable military force this country had ever seen, was being transported by water to the York Peninsula for an advance on the Confederate capital. Homer was in Washington on April 1st, saw and drew the troops embarking at Alexandria, and accompanied them on a transport to the peninsula. Here the army, under McClellan's overcautious command, was wasting a precious month besieging Yorktown. Homer was with the troops throughout the siege, his pencil constantly busy, making scores of sketches of soldiers reconnoitering, skirmishing, drilling, loafing under the hot Virginia sun. He remained until after the Confederate evacuation of the town on May 3rd; but he probably did not follow the troops in their advance up the peninsula, for there were no illustrations by him of this offensive phase of the campaign which brought them to within a few miles of Richmond —so close that they could hear its church bells, closer than any Union force was to get for two long years. Nor were there any drawings to indicate that he saw the bloody Seven Days' Battles that ended in McClellan's withdrawal and the failure of the campaign. Judging by his work in *Harper's,* he was probably back in New York not later than June 1st, with a portfolio of sketches that were to furnish him with material for some time to come.

This was the only period we know of when Homer acted as a "special artist" at the front in the usual sense—one who covered specific events and sent his drawings (on paper) back to the magazine to be redrawn by staff artists, instead of doing them on the block himself in New York. The result could not have pleased him; how much character was lost in the process is shown by a double-page spread engraved from sketches by himself and by *Harper's* regular artist, in which it is impossible to distinguish between them.

It was after his return to New York that Homer did the best of his few battle scenes—"The War for the Union, 1862—A Cavalry Charge" and "The War for the Union, 1862—A Bayonet Charge." The usual battle picture was a descriptive panorama, showing the terrain and the disposition of forces; the soldiers were handsome and heroic and quite correct in their uniforms, and, although there had to be a few shells bursting and men falling, the whole affair seemed rather academic. But Homer's two battle pieces take us right into the thick of things; we are there in the front line, meeting the trampling horses, the saber slash, the bayonet thrust. No other drawings in the magazine had approached these in their vivid sensation of the violence of battle. They show that if Homer had wanted to he could have been the most effective military illustrator of the time. *Harper's* did not exaggerate when it called "A Bayonet Charge" "one of the most spirited pictures ever published in this country."

But Homer did not go on to exploit his talents in this direction. Indeed, in the next few years he did less and less work for *Harper's*. This could not have been from lack of opportunity, for *Harper's* showed by the space they gave him and by their editorial comments that they thought highly of him. He had found a new medium—painting.

Strangely enough, the man who was to become one of the greatest American painters did not begin to paint seriously until he was almost twenty-seven, in late 1862. "His very first picture in oils," wrote a friend, "represented a 'Sharpshooter' seated in a brig top, aiming at a distant 'Reb,' a canvas about 16 by 20. I sat with him many days while he worked on it, and remember discussing with him how much he could ask for it. He decided not less than sixty dollars, as that was what *Harper's* paid him for a full page drawing on the wood." (He redrew the painting on the block for *Harper's*, which published it with the caption "The Army of the Potomac—A Sharp-shooter on Picket Duty.") This painting and another war picture—of which Homer later said, "It is about as beautiful and interesting as the button on a barn door"—he placed in an exhibition, telling his older brother Charles that if they were not sold he would give up painting and take a full-time job at *Harper's*. Charles bought them secretly, a fact which Winslow did not discover until years later, when he swore roundly and refused to speak to his brother for weeks.

In the meantime the number of his reportorial illustrations for *Harper's* had declined from eight in 1863 to four in 1864, three in 1865, none in 1866. After the Peninsular Campaign he never again illustrated specific events of the war, and his front-line subjects became fewer and fewer. There were none at all during the summer of 1863, which witnessed Gettysburg and some of the most critical days for the Union.

But he did visit the front again, probably several times. Pictures of camp life in winter appeared in 1863 and 1864. One of his paintings was based on sketches made on the battlefield during Grant's battering-ram advance through the Virginia forests in the spring of 1864. Another oil proves that he saw something of the siege of Petersburg in 1864, when the fighting took on the character of modern trench warfare. Other works indicate that he was present during the momentous spring days of 1865 when Lee's exhausted army finally abandoned Petersburg and began the retreat that ended in Appomattox. A quaint little drawing shows Lincoln and his son Tad waiting with Grant at the railroad station in City Point, at the beginning of that long chase.

# The Civil War

# HARPER'S WEEKLY.
## A JOURNAL OF CIVILIZATION

VOL. V.—No. 220.]     NEW YORK, SATURDAY, MARCH 16, 1861.     [PRICE FIVE CENTS.

Entered according to Act of Congress, in the Year 1861, by Harper & Brothers, in the Clerk's Office of the District Court for the Southern District of New York.

THE INAUGURAL PROCESSION AT WASHINGTON PASSING THE GATE OF THE CAPITOL GROUNDS.—FROM A SKETCH BY OUR SPECIAL ARTIST.—[SEE PAGE 165.]

THE INAUGURAL PROCESSION AT WASHINGTON
PASSING THE GATE OF THE CAPITOL GROUNDS
*Harper's Weekly*
March 16, 1861

51

THE INAUGURATION OF ABRAHAM LINCOLN AS PRESIDENT OF THE UNITED STATES, AT THE CAPITOL, WASHINGTON, MARCH 4, 1861    *Harper's Weekly*    March 16, 1861

THE SEVENTY-NINTH REGIMENT (HIGHLANDERS) NEW YORK STATE MILITIA     *Harper's Weekly*     May 25, 1861

53

54

THE WAR—MAKING HAVELOCKS
FOR THE VOLUNTEERS
*Harper's Weekly*
June 29, 1861

The bold soldier boy

THE GIRL I LEFT BEHIND ME

DIXIE

GLORY HALLELUJAH

CHRISTMAS BOXES IN CAMP—CHRISTMAS, 1861
*Harper's Weekly*
January 4, 1862

REBELS OUTSIDE THEIR WORKS AT YORKTOWN
RECONNOITRING WITH DARK LANTERNS
*Harper's Weekly*
May 17, 1862

THE WAR FOR THE UNION, 1862 — A CAVALRY CHARGE    *Harper's Weekly*    July 5, 1862

THE WAR FOR THE UNION, 1862—A BAYONET CHARGE  *Harper's Weekly*  July 12, 1862

61

THANKSGIVING IN CAMP    *Harper's Weekly*    November 29, 1862

THE ARMY OF THE POTOMAC—A SHARP-SHOOTER ON PICKET DUTY    *Harper's Weekly*    November 15, 1862

A SHELL IN THE REBEL TRENCHES    *Harper's Weekly*    January 17, 1863

WINTER-QUARTERS IN CAMP—THE INSIDE OF A HUT     *Harper's Weekly*     January 24, 1863

SENDING MONEY HOME

THE LETTER

A DESCENT ON THE SUTLER

PAY-DAY IN THE ARMY OF THE POTOMAC   *Harper's Weekly*   February 28, 1863

GREAT SUMTER MEETING IN UNION SQUARE, NEW YORK, APRIL 11, 1863    *Harper's Weekly*    April 25, 1863

THE APPROACH OF THE BRITISH PIRATE "ALABAMA"
*Harper's Weekly*
April 25, 1863

Cover of the portfolio *Campaign Sketches*
1863

THE BAGGAGE TRAIN
from the portfolio *Campaign Sketches*
1863

73

THE COFFEE CALL
from the portfolio *Campaign Sketches*
1863

OUR JOLLY COOK
from the portfolio *Campaign Sketches*
1863

75

FORAGING
from the portfolio *Campaign Sketches*
1863

A PASS TIME
from the portfolio *Campaign Sketches*
1863

THE LETTER FOR HOME
from the portfolio *Campaign Sketches*
1863

OUR SPECIAL    from the series *Life in Camp*    1864          GOOD BYE    from the series *Life in Camp*    1864

*78*

HALT OF A WAGON TRAIN    *Harper's Weekly*    February 6, 1864

"Any Thing for Me, if You Please?"—
Post-office of the Brooklyn Fair
in Aid of the Sanitary Commission
*Harper's Weekly*
March 5, 1864

Our Watering-places—The Empty Sleeve at Newport    *Harper's Weekly*    August 26, 1865

# France

As a young man Homer once said, "If a man wants to be an artist, he should never look at pictures." This can be put down to youthful bumptiousness, but it was somewhat true of his attitude all his life. Both his illustrations and his paintings show parallels to the schools and tendencies of his time: his illustrations, to the current Anglo-American graphic style; his early paintings, to the Barbizon School and French naturalism. But these similarities are very general, and it is hard to detect the influence of any particular school in his early work. His style is that of an artist who had looked more at nature than at art. It has a quality that is rare in the modern world: an innocent eye. He relied on his eyes more than on tradition, on what he saw more than on what others had taught him to see.

He did not go abroad until he was almost thirty-one, in late 1866. Ten months were spent in France, some partly in Paris, but probably more in the country. As far as we know he attended no art classes, but painted on his own. He must have visited the Louvre, for an illustration in *Harper's* shows the Long Gallery crowded with students copying the old masters; but there is no evidence that he joined them. How much he looked at the great paintings and what he thought of them are unknown.

Where he spent at least part of his time is shown by two *Harper's* illustrations of Paris dance halls. At the Mabille the cancan is being danced, the men in top hats, the girls kicking high; at the Casino the crowd surrounds a male dancer who is whirling his partner off her feet. These were scenes such as Toulouse-Lautrec was to picture twenty years later. They were strong meat for an American family journal, and *Harper's* felt it necessary to append a long censorious article, ending piously: "We shall not venture to look into the abyss on the brink of which these frenzied men and women are dancing, and this too curious crowd of spectators is treading. This is work for the severe and steady eye of the preacher and moralist."

Part of the time he had a studio in Montmartre, shared with a friend from Belmont who later recalled him as a genial young man who enjoyed the life of Paris. When Homer left in the fall of 1867 he was so broke that he had to borrow the fare from his friend, to whom he later gave the choice of any of his paintings.

This French experience left no great influence on his work, in either subjects or style—certainly not as much as on his younger American colleagues who were beginning to study in Paris. His paintings before he went abroad had already shown curious parallels to the works of the young French Impressionists, but without any possible influence, since the latter were still unknown in this country. Homer was an independent American pioneer of the Impressionistic viewpoint that was manifesting itself in several countries at this time.

But this French visit brought another experience: his first two long ocean voyages, as far as we know. The two-page illustration "Homeward-bound" reveals not only his eye for stylishness in both women and men, but also a love of ships and of the surging movement and wide skies of the deep sea—elements that were to become dominant in his later art.

France

ART-STUDENTS AND COPYISTS IN THE LOUVRE GALLERY, PARIS    *Harper's Weekly*    January 11, 1868

87

A PARISIAN BALL—DANCING AT THE MABILLE, PARIS    *Harper's Weekly*    November 23, 1867

A PARISIAN BALL—DANCING AT THE CASINO    *Harper's Weekly*    November 23, 1867

# The Illustrator as Artist

BEFORE HE LEFT FOR FRANCE Homer appeared to have abandoned illustrating in favor of painting. But after his return he took it up again, perhaps to recoup his finances. Indeed, for several years he supported himself chiefly as an illustrator. From 1868 to 1874 he was busier than ever in this field, not only for *Harper's Weekly* but also for other magazines, including *Harper's Bazaar, Appletons' Journal of Literature, Science, and Art, The Galaxy, Our Young Folks,* and *Hearth and Home.* When, in 1870, the Boston publishers of the staid *Every Saturday* changed it into a picture magazine along the lines of the New York ones, Homer deserted *Harper's Weekly* and gave the new venture all his work, including some of his finest illustrations. Not until it had once more been proved that Boston would not support an illustrated journal did he return to the fold. In the 1860's and 1870's he also illustrated a number of books, especially giftbook editions of the poems of Tennyson, Bryant, and the New England poets Whittier, Longfellow, Lowell, and Lucy Larcom.

In these years Homer led a double life, as illustrator and painter. In his paintings after the Civil War he had turned to the life he loved best, that of the country. Although New York was his winter home for over twenty years, he never painted it. The city itself, like most American cities of the time, had little to offer to a painter's eye: a big ugly town, monotonously rectangular, with muddy streets and hideous slums. To picture the New York of Boss Tweed's day required the pencil of a satirist, which Homer was far from being.

But one thing New York had for Homer the illustrator—the world of fashion and of femininity. We usually think of him as the hermit of his later years, living alone on the Maine coast and painting his epics of the sea and the wilderness. But in his thirties he was quite a different person: good-looking if not handsome, with a strong aquiline nose and handlebar moustache, and always well dressed, in the loud checked suits, starched collars, and bowler hats of the period. He had many friends and enjoyed social life, though never much of a talker. He was to remain a bachelor all his life, but a close friend said that "he had the usual number of love affairs as a young man."

From the first his illustrations showed an admiration for feminine beauty and a keen eye for fashion. Sometimes his young ladies were engaged in indoor social functions, as in the delightful "Waiting for Calls on New-year's Day." But more often he liked to show them outdoors in such winter activities as sleighing and skating. Particularly in his skating scenes, the elaborate creations of the dressmaker, swathing young bodies in graceful motion, created enchanting decorative patterns.

Occasionally (though only occasionally) there was a glimpse of the seamy side of city life, as in one of his last urban illustrations, "Station-house Lodgers," with its realistic exposé of human misery. Almost equally dreary was "Jurors Listening to Counsel, Supreme Court, New City Hall, New York." The juror at the extreme right bears a suspicious resemblance to the artist himself, and his deadpan boredom bears out Homer's statement in later years that he left New York for the solitude of Maine in order to escape jury duty.

Industrial labor found as little place in his work as in that of other illustrators of the day. "New England Factory Life—'Bell-time'" was a rare exception, as was the sympathetic and precisely drawn figure of the factory girl that illustrates Bryant's poem, *The Song of the Sower*. More to Homer's taste was the small rural factory beside the millpond in "The Morning Bell."

As the years passed, Homer's published work became less and less illustration in the usual meaning of the word. Occasionally he illustrated a story, novel, or poem, but he no longer did reportorial drawings of current events or persons. Nor did he pursue the humorous vein that had shown in some of his Civil War subjects. Though an element of quiet humor was often present, there was little satire or caricature, and in later years his rare attempts to be funny were usually failures. His few works which appear to have been commissioned, such as several of his city scenes, generally fall flat. He was always best in the subjects that he chose to please himself, and most of his publishers seem to have realized this and given him a free hand. His illustrations became pictures, as independent of text or topical interest as his paintings. Several, indeed, were actually reproductions of his oils, which he himself redrew on the block, such as "Snap-the-whip" and "High Tide." In his illustrations of these years—the late 1860's and early 1870's—he reached his highest point, in both content and style.

Homer's graphic style belonged in the Anglo-American tradition of the time in its sober naturalism, as contrasted with the greater plastic freedom and caricatural sense of French and German illustrators. Of the English school he was closest to his contemporaries Tenniel, Pinwell, and Sandys. While not so accomplished in academic technique, he showed fresher observation, stronger form, and a clearer sense of decorative values. In style as in subjects, the American and specifically the New England character of his work was unmistakable. In his illustrations for the works of such typically New England writers as Whittier, Lowell, and Lucy Larcom, one finds that rare happening, a complete rapport between writer and illustrator, and one regrets that he did not do more such books. A *Snowbound* illustrated by Homer would have been one of the classics of American bookmaking.

Wood-engraving is the simplest, most direct form of engraving. Essentially it is the same as printing from type: the raised surfaces print, instead of the incised lines as in etching, mezzotint, or intaglio engraving. The impression is in flat black, with no variation in tone. To produce tone, the engraver of Homer's time cut away the wood-block surface in fine lines, leaving parallel hairlines of black which gave a general effect of gray. Actually this was only an approximation of the tones of the artist's original drawing. But so skillful were the engravers of his day that they came remarkably close to interpreting the varied tones of a wash drawing in the unvarying flat black lines of wood-engraving.

Essentially a line medium, wood-engraving—while using tone—had to retain its basically linear character. In the hands of the best illustrators of the time, who respected its nature—in America, men such as Darley, Nast, Abbey, Frost, and Homer—it was a beautiful medium. The very flatness of its blacks and whites gave it a decorative quality and made it harmonize perfectly with type.

Homer's artistry and technical skill grew with the years. While he used tone more and more, until most of his work of the 1870's was in full tone, he seldom lost sight of the linear basis of wood-engraving. The composition was built on a strong line drawing; tone served as an enrichment but remained subordinate. Outlines were bold, and lights and shadows were sharply defined. Everything was clear-cut, with no trying for soft effects. A certain severity in his style accorded well with the character of the medium, as did the largeness of his forms and his ability to simplify, to concentrate on essentials. His instinctive sense of design, of the rhythmic play of lines, of the relations of dark and light areas and the patterns they create—a sense that had shown in his work from the beginning—became clearer and more conscious with the years. His finest illustrations combined skillful representation with decorative values of a high order. An interesting parallel to Japanese art was apparent. It had appeared in his paintings and illustrations before he went abroad, such as the handsome skating scene in *Leslie's* of January, 1866. Probably the influence had come to him through his friend, the painter John La Farge, who was collecting Japanese prints in the early 1860's. But Homer's affinity to Oriental art was never as conscious or deliberate as was the case with Whistler. It was rather a parallel in ways of seeing nature, and of translating nature's facts into design.

# The Illustrator as Artist

97

WAITING FOR CALLS ON NEW-YEAR'S DAY    *Harper's Bazaar*    January 2, 1869

OUR NATIONAL WINTER EXERCISE—SKATING    *Frank Leslie's Illustrated Newspaper*    January 13, 1866

99

CUTTING A FIGURE  *Every Saturday*  February 4, 1871

"Winter"—A Skating Scene    *Harper's Weekly*    January 25, 1868

OPENING DAY IN NEW YORK    *Harper's Bazaar*    March 21, 1868

THE MORNING WALK—YOUNG LADIES' SCHOOL PROMENADING THE AVENUE    *Harper's Weekly*    March 28, 1868

FIRE-WORKS ON THE NIGHT OF THE FOURTH OF JULY    *Harper's Weekly*    July 11, 1868

JURORS LISTENING TO COUNSEL, SUPREME COURT, NEW CITY HALL, NEW YORK    *Harper's Weekly*    February 20, 1869

106

THE CHINESE IN NEW YORK—
SCENE IN A BAXTER STREET CLUB-HOUSE
*Harper's Weekly*
March 7, 1874

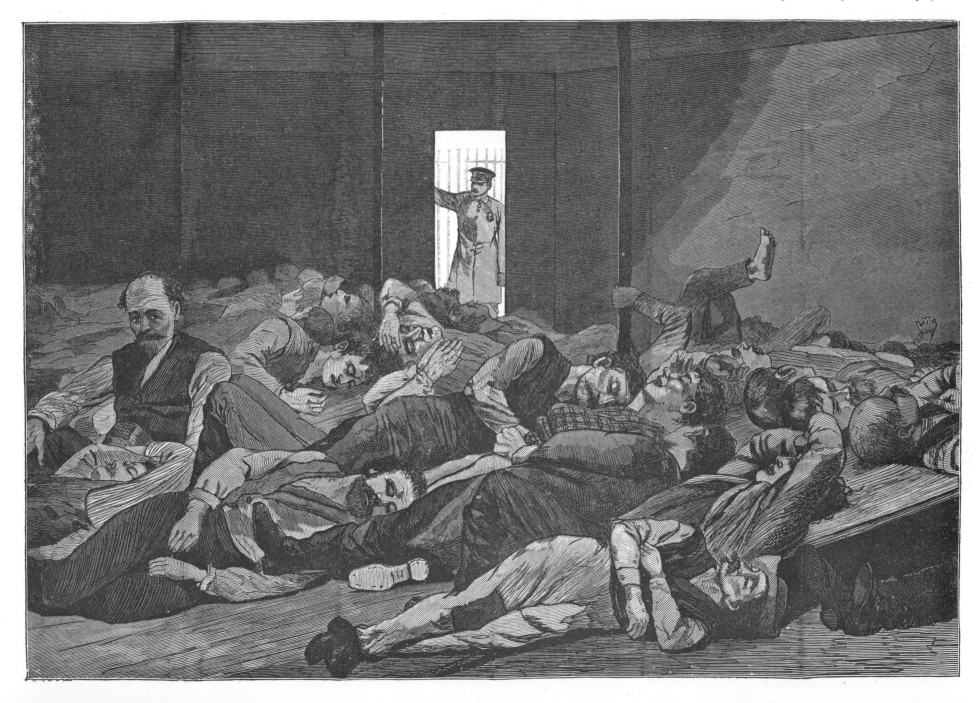

THE WATCHMAN.

NINE O'CLOCK BELL.

THE TOWER.

A FIRE.

WATCH-TOWER,
CORNER OF SPRING AND VARICK STREETS, NEW YORK
*Harper's Weekly*
February 28, 1874

THE MORNING BELL    *Harper's Weekly*    December 13, 1873

"... for those who throw
The clanking shuttle to and fro"
from the book *Song of the Sower*    1871

# Summer Resorts and Recreations

FROM HIS BOYHOOD Homer loved the country and outdoor life. He was a born wanderer, settling for a few weeks or months in some new place on the seashore, in the mountains, or in the deep country. New York remained his winter residence, but with the late spring he would be on the move, painting and drawing throughout New England and eastern New York State, sometimes into Pennsylvania and south to Virginia and North Carolina. These summer months away from the city furnished material for all his paintings and most of his illustrations.

A favorite field was the world of summer resorts: the seaside resorts of Massachusetts, Long Island, and New Jersey, and the mountain resorts of the White Mountains, the Catskills, and the Adirondacks. In all these summer scenes women played the leading roles. After the languors of the mid-Victorian era, American women were enjoying increasing physical freedom. Compared to their predecessors of the Currier & Ives period, Homer's women were young amazons, riding, bathing, playing croquet, going on picnics and straw rides—recreations still ladylike but less inhibited than those of former days. In his pictures they play croquet in hoopskirts, against gentlemen in bowler hats. They ride up the Mount Washington carriage road—sidesaddle, of course—in billowy white skirts. At Long Branch—then the fashionable summer residence of President Grant—they descend the stairs down the bluffs, the sea breeze raising havoc with their many-flounced skirts. Or, swathed in all-concealing bathing suits down to long pantaloons and stockings, they pose on the beach, only to emerge from the water as sodden, dripping bundles.

Bathing was still considered somewhat risqué. An article accompanying "Bathing at Long Branch" in *Every Saturday* spoke of the "three young girls, ... clad in perfectly fitting garments of bright colored flannel," and went on to comment: "The question, to bathe or not to bathe in public, will always remain an open one. By taking proper precautions one can be pretty sure of not outraging the proprieties, but of not making oneself a ridiculous object,—a spectacle to be derided and howled at,—who can be sure?" Homer himself felt differently, for even his bedraggled bathing beauties, while pictured with complete veracity, manage to look charming. In his painting "High Tide" he even dared to show two of them with short pantaloons and no stockings, which led one critic to say that the picture was "perhaps not quite refined." (In his redrawing of the painting for *Every Saturday* the pantaloons have once more descended to the ankles.)

The girls were all young and attractive in their various ways—the dashing, romantic brunette, the buxom blonde of the strongly Anglo-Saxon type that Homer particularly favored. Seldom do we see an older woman or a plain one. He tended to make them types rather than individuals—the Homer Girl, like the later Gibson Girl—though he never idealized them to the extent that his contemporaries did. They were neither icy goddesses nor ethereal visions, but human beings. Without seductiveness or coyness, they had the air of mingled innocence and independence that marked the young American woman of the period. Whatever sentiment he revealed was extremely reserved. For all his preoccupation with women, a certain detachment was apparent; he pictured them as supremely decorative creatures rather than as strongly individualized persons. The eye's pleasure in the sight of attractive women, stylishly dressed and engaged in pleasant activities, was enough for him.

With his sense of fashion, he delighted in the hoopskirts, flounces, puffed sleeves, little round pillboxes, flying ribbons, and all the other charming absurdities of this unstreamlined day. Where less realistic artists toned down these extremes of fashion, he exploited their decorative possibilities to the full, though with no hint of caricature. In his work one can follow not only changes in style but also the subtler differences between the clothes of the Long Branch belle and her simpler country sister. As the *Nation* said of his paintings in 1866: "As regards costume alone, these pictures ought to be taken care of, that our descendants may see how the incredible female dress of the present day actually did look, when worn by active young women."

Homer was one of the first to picture the actual contemporary American girl, who has since become so favorite a subject for our artists and writers. She has seldom had a more sympathetic, yet at the same time more honest, interpreter. The works in which she figures, with their engaging mixture of candor and elegance, are the most delightful pictorial record of fashionable American country life of the period.

In several of the illustrations and paintings of the early 1870's appears a brown-haired girl with dark eyes and a vivacious face full of character. In "High Tide" she is seated on the beach fastening her bathing shoe. Homer family legend says that she was the object of the young artist's most serious love affair. Because of his reticence her name and the whole story will never be known, except that the affair seems to have ended unhappily because he did not have the income to marry. As far as we know, no other woman ever took her place. By middle life Homer was a confirmed bachelor.

This experience unquestionably had a deep effect on his attitude toward women and society. In his youth, though reserved, he had led a normal social life. From this time on he became more and more unsociable. His unhappy love affair was undoubtably a factor—though by no means the only one—in his later abandonment of city life for the solitude of the Maine coast. From then on the few women he pictured were no longer the elegant young ladies of his earlier work, but sturdy outdoor types, as robust as men, with hardly a trace of femininity.

# Summer Resorts and Recreations

WHAT SHALL WE DO NEXT?     *Harper's Bazaar*     July 31, 1869

THE COOLEST SPOT IN NEW ENGLAND—
SUMMIT OF MOUNT WASHINGTON
*Harper's Bazaar*
July 23, 1870

THE STRAW RIDE    *Harper's Bazaar*    September 25, 1869

# Appletons' Journal

### OF LITERATURE SCIENCE AND ART.

ENTERED, according to Act of Congress, in the year 1869, by D. APPLETON & CO., in the Clerk's Office of the District Court of the United States for the Southern District of New York.

No. 17.—WITH SUPPLEMENT]     SATURDAY, JULY 24, 1869.     [PRICE TEN CENTS.

ON THE ROAD TO LAKE GEORGE. BY WINSLOW HOMER.

ON THE ROAD TO LAKE GEORGE
*Appletons' Journal of Literature, Science, and Art*
July 24, 1869

128

Low Tide    *Every Saturday*    August 6, 1870

129

HIGH TIDE    *Every Saturday*    August 6, 1870

ON THE BLUFF AT LONG BRANCH, AT THE BATHING HOUR    *Harper's Weekly*    August 6, 1870

131

ON THE BEACH—TWO ARE COMPANY, THREE ARE NONE    *Harper's Weekly*    August 17, 1872

THE BATHERS
*Harper's Weekly*
August 2, 1873

AT THE SPRING: SARATOGA
*Hearth and Home*
August 28, 1869

A QUIET DAY IN THE WOODS
*Appletons' Journal of Literature, Science, and Art*
June 25, 1870

THE ROBIN'S NOTE
*Every Saturday*
August 20, 1870

HOMER

UNDER THE FALLS, CATSKILL MOUNTAINS     *Harper's Weekly*     September 14, 1872

A Country Store,—Getting Weighed   *Every Saturday*   March 25, 1871

# The Farm

More often than the fashionable world of summer resorts, Homer pictured a simpler kind of country life—that of the farm, of the deep country and its year-round natives. These illustrations form a cycle of the seasons: spring, a farmer grafting an apple tree; summer, a haymaker pausing in the midday heat for a drink of water; autumn, two boys husking corn amid the corn shocks and pumpkins strewn among the stubbles of a harvested field; winter, young men digging a path from their farmhouse through shoulder-high snow.

Here were plain, prosaic scenes from everyday farm life, with no trace of the sentimental idealization of everything rural that was usual among the genre painters and printmakers of the time. The men and women—with their spare, uncouth bodies, their straw hats, calico sunbonnets, flannel shirts, and cowhide boots—were pictured without either sweetening or caricature, but with the truth that comes from firsthand observation. And their surroundings were depicted with the same candor: farms with bare wooden houses and barns, rail fences, tumbledown stone walls, and orchards of gnarled old fruit trees, all seen in the clear air and strong sunlight of the American climate. These homely scenes were represented with no attempt to make them look like the mellow European countryside, but with a sure grasp of the character of the American land.

On the other hand, the accent was on the healthy, pleasant side of country existence; Homer did not show the unending labor, the bent back, the abandoned farm. He was picturing American farm life in its golden day, focusing on its cheer, self-reliance, and simple recreations. His honest realism was mingled with a strain of idyllic poetry, a reserved but deeply felt attachment to this life spent close to the earth, in daily contact with nature. The character and flavor of the old American farm life has never been captured with more utter authenticity, or more love.

It was this complete truthfulness that both fascinated and revolted young Henry James, who was about to abandon the United States for Europe. "He is barbarously simple," James wrote of Homer's paintings of the time, "and, to our eye, he is horribly ugly; but there is nevertheless something one likes about him. What is it? For ourselves, it is not his subjects. We frankly confess that we detest his subjects. . . . He has chosen the least pictorial features of the least pictorial range of scenery and civilization; he has resolutely treated them as if they *were* pictorial; . . . and to reward his audacity, he has incontestably succeeded."

# The Farm

THE DINNER HORN
*Harper's Weekly*
June 11, 1870

146

**MAKING HAY**  *Harper's Weekly*  July 6, 1872

147

SPRING FARM WORK — GRAFTING
*Harper's Weekly*
April 30, 1870

THE LAST DAYS OF HARVEST    *Harper's Weekly*    December 6, 1873

PUMPKINS AMONG THE CORN    *Scribner's Monthly*    August, 1878

149

A WINTER-MORNING,—SHOVELLING OUT    *Every Saturday*    January 14, 1871

from the book *Rural Poems*    1869

"As there, with comely steps, up hill
She rose by elm-trees, all in ranks."

"As he may stand and knock with shaking hand,
And lean to hear the sweetest voice inside."

title page

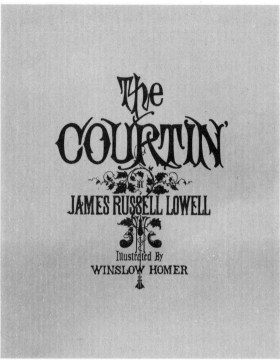

"Zekle crep' up quite unbeknown
An' peeked in thru' the winder."

"Says he, 'I'd better call agin.' "

"An' . . . . Wal, he up an' kist her."

"There sot Huldy all alone,
　　　'Ith no one nigh to hender."

"You want to see my Pa, I s'pose?"

"An' teary roun' the lashes."

"In meetin' come nex' Sunday."

# Childhood

MANY OF HOMER'S COUNTRY SCENES were devoted to children. We see them sitting on the hard benches of a one-room rural school, presided over by a pretty teacher. Released from school, a row of barefoot boys races across a field to "snap the whip" and send those at the end tumbling head over heels. They swing on birch trees, pick green apples, gather blackberries, shake down chestnuts, rifle strawberry beds, trap birds, raid sand-swallow nests, fish for suckers among the lily pads of a pond, and explore all the other delights of childhood in the country.

Homer's boys and girls were no little Victorian angels, but healthy children full of energy and adventurousness. He never condescended to them. He himself had preserved in manhood the pleasures of his own country boyhood, never allowing civilization to dull their keen edge. There was no element of nostalgia in all this, no mourning for lost childhood; he was presenting with firsthand enjoyment the things that make childhood memorable—the child's joy in freedom and adventure, in oneness with nature. The world had an early-morning freshness, a sense of unexplored delight. Not that such feelings were openly expressed; his style remained objective. But this very matter-of-factness, this concern with things rather than emotions, was close to a boy's outlook. His art presents the world as a boy saw and felt it, pictured with a man's grasp of actuality. Complete sympathy with childhood was united with complete unsentimentality.

This self-identification with childhood could also be found among the American writers of the time. Amid the raw realities of the newly industrialized United States, many of our authors remained attached to the simpler world of their youth. *Little Women*, appearing in 1868, ushered in a series of remarkable books about children: *Tom Sawyer* and *Huckleberry Finn*, Thomas Bailey Aldrich's *Story of a Bad Boy*, Charles Dudley Warner's *Being a Boy*, Lucy Larcom's *Childhood Songs*. Passages in them read like Homer's pictures put into words. While there is no exact literary equivalent to his art, it is nearest to Mark Twain's combination of drastic realism and deep personal emotion.

# Childhood

157

SPRING BLOSSOMS    *Harper's Weekly*    May 21, 1870

WATCHING THE CROWS    *Our Young Folks*    June, 1868

SWINGING ON A BIRCH-TREE    *Our Young Folks*    June, 1867

GREEN APPLES     *Our Young Folks*     August, 1868

THE BIRD-CATCHERS     *Our Young Folks*     August, 1867

THE STRAWBERRY BED     *Our Young Folks*     July, 1868

159

CHESTNUTTING
*Every Saturday*
October 29, 1870

162

THE NOONING    *Harper's Weekly*    August 16, 1873

*163*

"Snap-the-whip"    *Harper's Weekly*    September 20, 1873

WATER-MELON EATERS     *Art Journal*     August, 1878

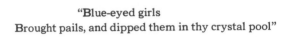

"Blue-eyed girls
Brought pails, and dipped them in thy crystal pool"

GATHERING WILD BLACKBERRIES    *Scribner's Monthly*    April, 1880

"And children, ruddy-cheeked and flaxen-haired,
Gathering the glistening cowslip from thy edge."

"Shouting boys, let loose
For a wild holiday, have quaintly shaped
Into a cup the folded linden-leaf,
And dipped thy sliding crystal."

167

# Gloucester, 1873-1874

CURIOUSLY ENOUGH, it was not until he was thirty-seven that Homer began to make full use of the medium of which he was to become a master: watercolor. The medium suited him perfectly. Always essentially a draftsman and a recorder of the outdoor world, in watercolor he could work directly from nature, from the first pencil indications to the finished picture in color. Within a few years watercolor was to replace illustration as his second medium—his first, of course, being oil.

The summer of 1873 he spent in the fishing port of Gloucester, Massachusetts, painting a series of watercolors of the life of the harbor: shipbuilding, fishing schooners coming and going, and, especially, children—rowing, sailing, fishing, swimming, playing around the wharves, and picking berries in the rocky pastures of Cape Ann. Among all his lifework these first watercolors have a special quality. They express with directness and simple purity the freshness of life's morning, and childhood's unclouded joy in summer and sunlight and the sea.

On these watercolors, and on sketches in oil and pencil, Homer based a series of drawings for *Harper's Weekly* in 1873 and 1874 which were his culminating achievements in illustration. He composed them with particular care, using several sketches for each, and taking parts of them and combining them. For example, "Ship-building, Gloucester Harbor" was made up from two small oils—one of the ship, another of the two boys in the foreground—

and a watercolor of the group of boys at the left. The result was a composition more complete than any of them. "Gathering Berries" was a repetition (in reverse) of "The Berry Pickers," one of his most delightful watercolors, but the composition was much improved by the addition of the girl in the left foreground.

These 1873 and 1874 illustrations are among his most thoughtfully designed works, comparable to the finest of his mature paintings. They are also among the best-engraved of his illustrations, for American engravers had gained greatly in skill since the 1850's and Homer himself had learned how to combine strong, precise draftsmanship with tonal values of a wide range and a fine delicacy.

At the height of his popularity as an illustrator, Homer suddenly stopped. After 1874 he did only one illustration for *Harper's Weekly*—"The Battle of Bunker Hill—Watching the Fight from Copp's Hill, in Boston," marking the one-hundredth anniversary of the event—and only a few illustrations for other magazines. Just why he gave up his career as an illustrator will never be known. The likeliest reason is that in watercolor he had discovered a richer medium, with the added virtue of color; and that the almost immediate success of his watercolors gave him an income to take the place of that from illustrating.

169

# Gloucester, 1873-1874

171

SEA-SIDE SKETCHES—A CLAM-BAKE     *Harper's Weekly*     August 23, 1873

GLOUCESTER HARBOR    *Harper's Weekly*    September 27, 1873

SHIP-BUILDING, GLOUCESTER HARBOR    *Harper's Weekly*    October 11, 1873

RAID ON A SAND-SWALLOW COLONY—
"HOW MANY EGGS?"
*Harper's Weekly*
June 13, 1874

175

SEESAW—GLOUCESTER, MASSACHUSETTS     *Harper's Weekly*     September 12, 1874

177

GATHERING BERRIES     *Harper's Weekly*     July 11, 1874

# The Forest and the Sea

IN HOMER'S LATER CAREER AS A PAINTER, his two dominant themes became the forest and the sea. Both these great motifs were foretold in his illustrations of the 1870's.

His active outdoor life continued well into old age. He and his brother Charles spent many summers camping, fishing, and hunting in the Adirondacks, and later in the wilds of Quebec. Of Winslow as an angler, Charles said, "He did not go in for expensive or elaborate tackle, but he usually caught the biggest fish." These excursions, while mostly for sport, were always combined with painting.

At least as early as 1870 he was in the Adirondacks, still largely virgin wilderness undiscovered by the summer boarder. This trip resulted in a series of illustrations of life in the north woods, few in number but among his strongest.

The sea has always played an essential part in the life and mind of New England and of her sons. Homer's love of the sea came to him through his ancestry, and through his boyhood and youth in the seaport of Boston. How much of his childhood was spent on the water we do not know, but that he knew boats and ships and everything nautical with almost professional thoroughness is proved by his pictures.

Strangely enough, however, this devotion to salt water did not show itself fully in his work until his summer at Gloucester in 1873, and then it was the quiet water of the harbor rather than the deep sea. But before that the ocean had been the theme of a few illustrations, such as the vivid "Winter at Sea—Taking in Sail off the Coast" and the tragic "Wreck of the 'Atlantic'—Cast up by the Sea." The latter was prophetic of his later sea pictures in its revelation of the danger of the ocean, and in the heroic mold of the woman's figure.

It was not until he was forty-five that the sea became a major element in Homer's work. In 1881 and 1882 he spent two seasons on the east coast of England, painting the stormy North Sea and the hardy men and women who wrested their living from it. After his return to the United States he left New York for good, and settled on a lonely peninsula in Maine, Prout's Neck, within a stone's throw of the Atlantic. Here he was to live the rest of his life, entirely alone. And here his art reached full maturity, in the elemental poetry of his images of the northern wilderness, and in the thunderous power of his great marines.

# The Forest and the Sea

AT SEA,—SIGNALLING A PASSING STEAMER  *Every Saturday*  April 8, 1871

184

**TRAPPING IN THE ADIRONDACKS**    *Every Saturday*    December 24, 1870

CAMPING OUT IN THE ADIRONDACK MOUNTAINS    *Harper's Weekly*    November 7, 1874

LUMBERING IN WINTER
*Every Saturday*
January 28, 1871

J.P. DAVIS Sc.

187

188

WINTER AT SEA—TAKING IN SAIL OFF THE COAST     *Harper's Weekly*     January 16, 1869

THE WRECK OF THE "ATLANTIC"—CAST UP BY THE SEA    *Harper's Weekly*    April 26, 1873

# Index of Illustrations

This index of the illustrations by Winslow Homer which are reproduced in this book is arranged in three categories: periodicals, books, and lithographs. Within each category, the publications are arranged in alphabetical order. Individual illustrations from each periodical are listed in chronological order; those from each book are listed in the order in which they appear in the book. The place of publication is New York unless otherwise stated.

## PERIODICALS

## ACKNOWLEDGMENT

The publisher is grateful to Bernhardt Crystal of the Washington Irving Gallery, whose enthusiastic appreciation of the illustrations of Winslow Homer was the moving cause for the preparation of the present volume. In addition, Mr. Crystal kindly made available his own collection of Homer illustrations, which served as a major source for the reproductions appearing herein.

The publisher is also grateful to Lloyd Goodrich and the following institutions, who made available other original material needed in the preparation of this volume: Brooklyn Public Library; The Library of Congress, Washington, D.C.; The Metropolitan Museum of Art, New York; Museum of Fine Arts, Boston; The New York Public Library; The Whitney Museum of American Art, New York; and Yale University Library, New Haven.